NO
FUCKING
WAY

Pay
Me
Dammit

Face Meet Palm

Out
Of
Spoons

Where's
The
Eject
Button

Why
Even
Bother

WHAT
A
DISASTER

Beyond
All
Reason

Dodged
One
Hit
Another

In
The
Deep
End

In The Twilight Zone

Drive
Me
Crazy!

This
Wifi
Is
Shitty

Hell
No
Not
Again

Fucking
Office
Politics

Chasing
My
Tail

Just
Need
An
Out

Just
Shut
Up

Hold
The
Madness!

On The Edge Here!

HOLY
SHIT
AGAIN!

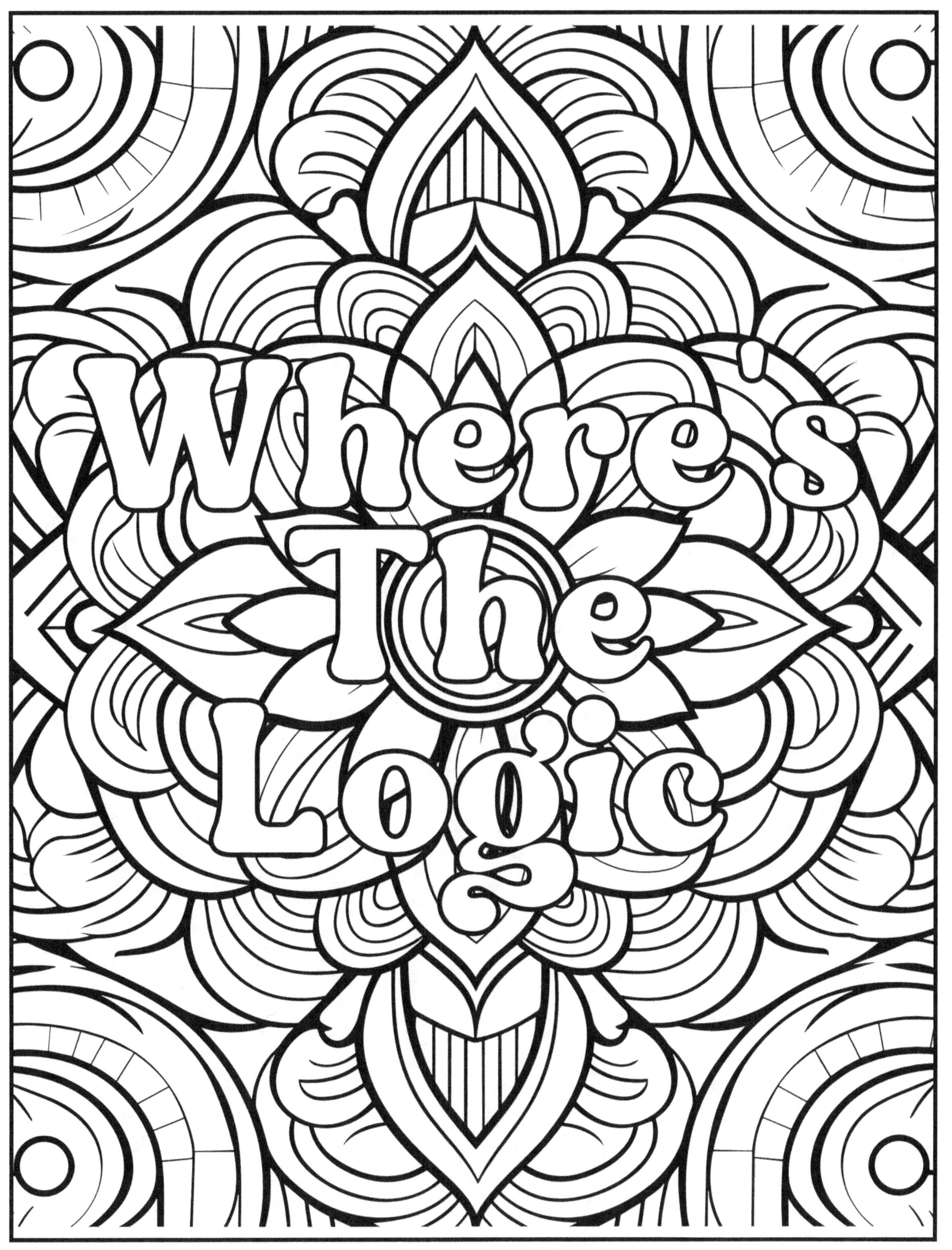

Where's
The
Logic

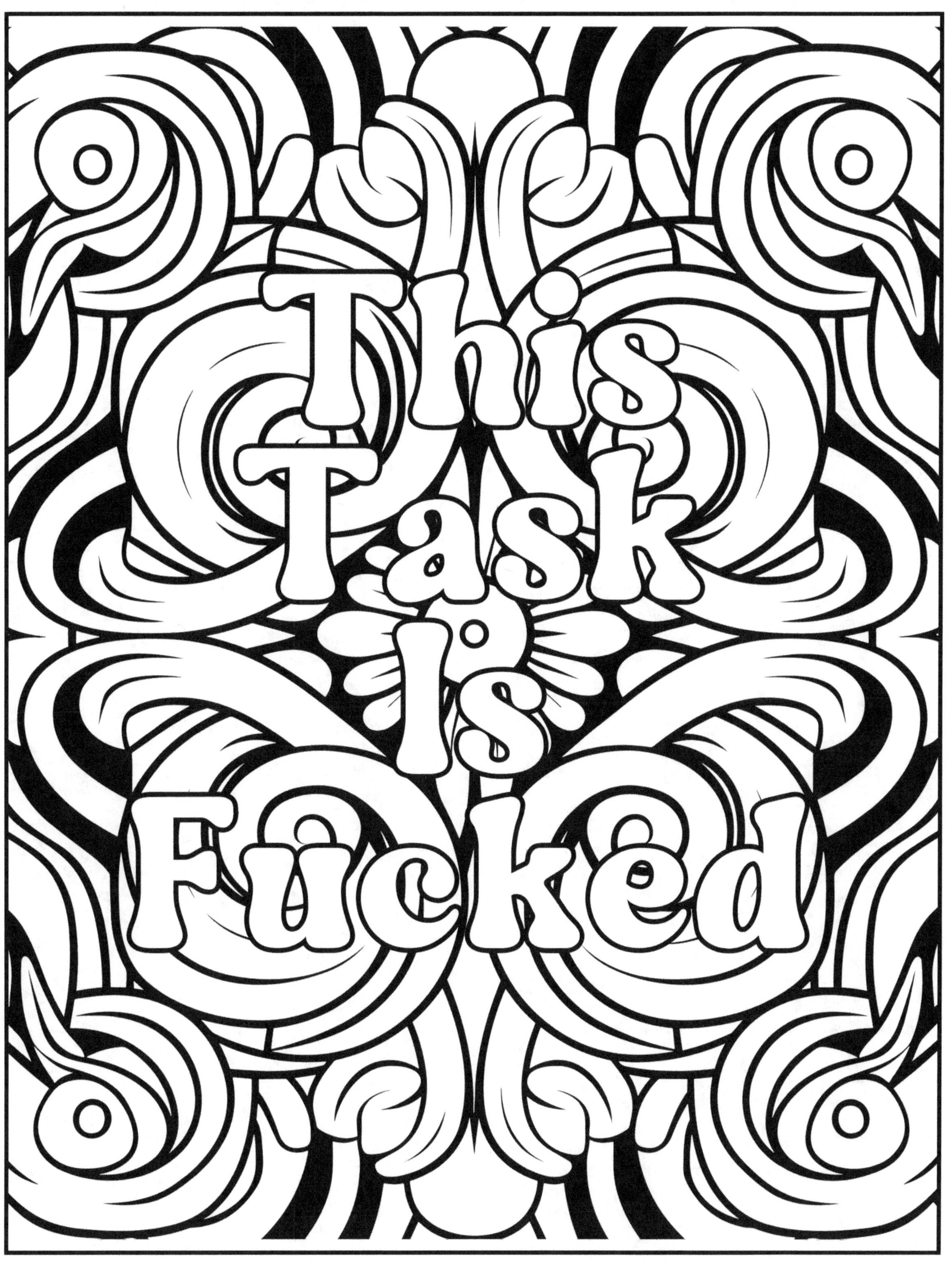

This
Task
Is
Fucked

No More
Goddamn
Emails

Quit
Your
Bitching

Mind In A Muddle

I
Need
A
New
Job

STRANGER
THAN
FICTION

Did I
Ask
For
This

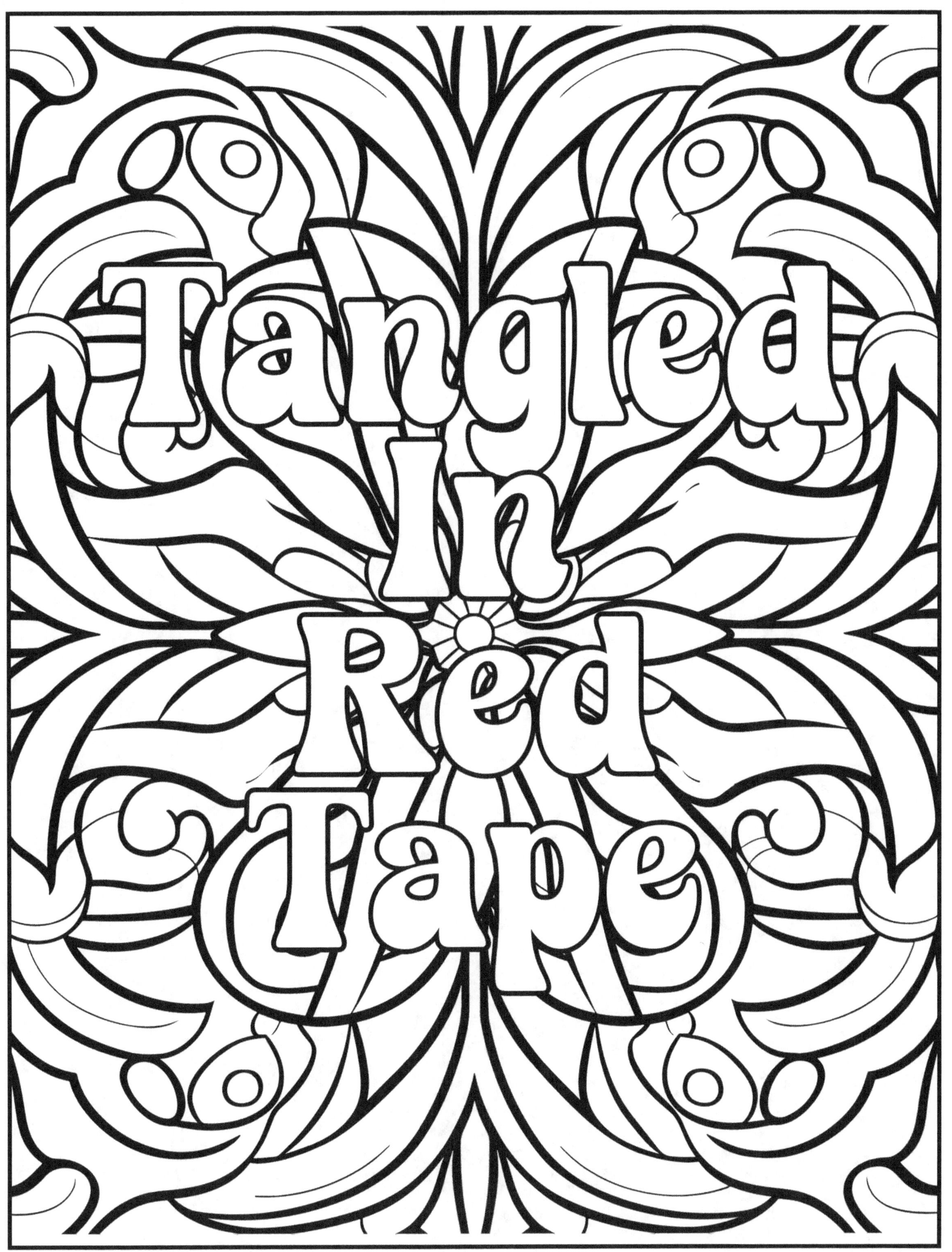
Tangled In Red Tape

Not
My
Problem

Almost
Had
It!

WHO
GIVES
A
FUCK

Not
In
The
Brochure

This Can't Be Right

Why
The
Secrecy

Is
This
A
Joke

More Of The Same Chaos

Going
Off
The
Rails

Back
To
The
Drawing
Board

WHO
EVEN
CARES

I
CAN'T
EVEN

Another
Dumbass
Idea

IS
THERE
AN
OFF
SWITCH

www.ingramcontent.com/pod-product-compliance
Lightning Source LLC
Chambersburg PA
CBHW080938260726
48661CB00010B/3981